under the
OCEAN

BY

PAUL BENNETT

UNDER THE OCEAN

Life can be found everywhere in the oceans, from the shallow, sunlit upper waters to the darkest depths. This makes the oceans by far the largest habitat in our world. They cover most of the Earth's surface, yet they are mostly unexplored because of their sheer vastness and power. The frightening sea monsters that the early sailors claimed had attacked their ships on long voyages were certainly flights of fancy. But as you will discover, there are certainly monstrous-looking creatures living in the salty depths. The oceans teem with life. Some sea creatures are tiny. For example, you would need a microscope to see phytoplankton (types of algae that form the basis of all life in the oceans). Others are huge—the blue whale is the largest creature ever to have lived. It grows to over 98 feet (30 meters) and weighs over 150 tons. It is now an endangered species due to overhunting in the past.

NOT JUST A FRIENDLY FACE

The bottlenose dolphin seems to have a knowing smile on its face. It is a very intelligent animal, able to "talk" to others of its kind with a wide range of grunts, whistles, and clicks. Dolphins, like whales, are not fish but mammals, which means they feed their young on milk.

WEIRD & WONDERFUL

The leafy sea dragon is just one of the unlikely-looking creatures of the oceans. It is, in fact, a type of sea horse, which is a small fish. Although it is a poor swimmer, it is well adapted to its life in the beds of seaweed that grow in the shallow waters of Australasia. The festoon of leaf-like flaps along its body act as camouflage, making it hard for a predator to spot it among the seaweed.

PLANET OCEAN

From space, the Earth appears blue because of the oceans, which cover nearly three-quarters of its surface. Water is essential for life; it was in the early oceans that life on our planet began. The oceans hide landscapes more varied and spectacular than those found on dry land. There are vast and towering mountain ranges, plunging, gash-like trenches in the ocean bed, and wide plains stretching for thousands of square miles. Instead of "Planet Earth," perhaps our world should be called "Planet Ocean."

SPEED & POWER

A black marlin leaps high out of the water. Its power and shape make it one of the high-speed swimmers of the ocean. Its snout is extended into a sharp spike, cutting through the water with little resistance, and its streamlined body tapers gently until it meets the curved tail. To feed, it dives into shoals of fish, attacking them at high speed with remarkable precision.

GENTLE GIANT

Despite its huge size, the humpback whale is completely harmless to humans. At 52 feet (16 m) in length, and weighing in at a hefty 65 tons, it is a graceful swimmer, using its large flippers to move its huge bulk with ease. Humpback whales are baleen whales, because of the bristles, or baleen, that hang in rows from the top of their mouths. The baleen acts as a strainer, trapping food, such as small fish or krill, after the whale has expelled a huge mouthful of water.

UNDERWATER GARDENS

Coral reefs teem with life. They grow only in warm water that is clean, shallow, and receives sufficient light. The majority of reefs are found around the tropics where there is a rocky platform not too far below the surface. Many of the fish that live among the corals have flat bodies that allow them to swim into, or through, the reef's many cracks and crevices.

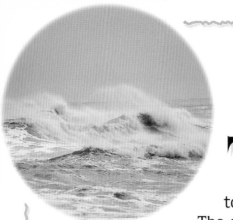

OCEANS OF THE WORLD

There are five oceans around the world—the Pacific, Atlantic, Indian, Southern, and Arctic Oceans—all linked together to form a single, large mass of salt water. The oceans are joined to seas, but these cover a smaller area than the oceans and are shallower. The Mediterranean, for example, a large inland sea between southern Europe and North Africa, is linked to the Atlantic Ocean by the Strait of Gibraltar. The oceans affect the weather and climate. The gravity of the sun and moon cause the tides. Ocean currents have an important influence on the movement of plankton and large marine animals.

THE ATLANTIC OCEAN

The Atlantic Ocean is the second largest ocean in the world. It separates North and South America in the west, from Europe and Africa in the east. A current, called the Gulf Stream, carries warm water from the tropics northward to the coast of Norway, where it stops the sea from freezing. Underneath the ocean is a vast mountain range called the Mid-Atlantic Ridge that is longer than the Himalayas.

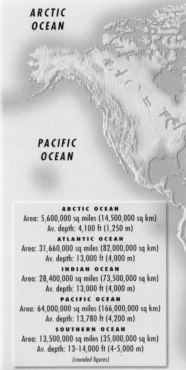

ARCTIC OCEAN

PACIFIC OCEAN

ATLA OC

ARCTIC OCEAN
Area: 5,600,000 sq miles (14,500,000 sq km)
Av. depth: 4,100 ft (1,250 m)
ATLANTIC OCEAN
Area: 31,660,000 sq miles (82,000,000 sq km)
Av. depth: 13,000 ft (4,000 m)
INDIAN OCEAN
Area: 28,400,000 sq miles (73,500,000 sq km)
Av. depth: 13,000 ft (4,000 m)
PACIFIC OCEAN
Area: 64,000,000 sq miles (166,000,000 sq km)
Av. depth: 13,780 ft (4,200 m)
SOUTHERN OCEAN
Area: 13,500,000 sq miles (35,000,000 sq km)
Av. depth: 13-14,000 ft (4-5,000 m)
(rounded figures)

THE SOUTHERN OCEAN

Formed by the southern reaches of the Pacific, Atlantic, and Indian Oceans, this ocean surrounds Antarctica, a large area of snow and ice-covered land at the South Pole. The rich, chilly water supports a wide variety of life, including this crabeater seal, which has jagged teeth for sieving krill, the small, shrimp-like creatures on which it feeds.

THE ARCTIC OCEAN

The Arctic is a partly-frozen ocean that lies to the north of North America, Asia, and Europe. In the summer months, much of the pack ice melts, reducing the area covered by sea ice. In addition, great chunks of ice plunge into the sea from the ends of glaciers around Greenland, and float away as towering icebergs.

ARCTIC OCEAN

PACIFIC OCEAN

INDIAN OCEAN

SOUTHERN OCEAN

THE PACIFIC OCEAN

This is the largest and deepest of the oceans, with an area that is more than double that of the Atlantic Ocean. "Pacific" means peaceful but, in fact, this ocean has some of the most violent sea and weather conditions of anywhere in the world, with destructive tropical storms and tsunamis (tidal waves). These are caused by volcanic activity and earthquakes on the ocean bed.

THE INDIAN OCEAN

This is an ocean of extremes, with a climate that ranges from warm and tropical in the north, to icy-cold where it meets the waters of the Southern Ocean. Dotted across the ocean are groups of beautiful islands. This is Kaafu Atoll in the Maldives, part of a string of coral islands to the southwest of India.

LAYERS OF LIFE

Scientists divide up the oceans into broad layers, or zones, so that if you took a trip down to the bottom of the ocean in a submersible (a type of deep-diving submarine) you would see the sunlit upper waters giving way to the twilight zone at about 650 feet (200 meters). Here the waters are poorly lit and the temperature of the water starts to drop rapidly. Below 3,280 feet (1,000 meters) you would enter the dark zone of the deep sea where no light penetrates. Deeper still are the abyss and the trenches. The Mariana Trench of the western Pacific is the deepest recorded sea trench at 36,200 feet (11,034 meters).

IN SHALLOW WATERS

Whether near the shore or out in the open ocean, animals and plants are most abundant in the well-lit shallow depths.

IN THE TWILIGHT ZONE

Below the shallow waters are the shady depths of the twilight zone. Life is less common here compared to the sunlit upper waters, but still more abundant then the blackness of the deep ocean. Types of animals found here, such as these sponges, can also be seen at other depths. Sponges are not free swimming but are attached to the same spot nearly all of their lives. Creatures such as these are called sessile animals.

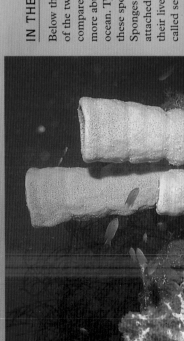

FLYING FISH

Out in the open ocean flying fish can be found. They can generate enough speed underwater to leap out of the water and, using their wing-like fins, glide through the air for 30 seconds or more to escape enemies.

THE DEEP OCEAN

Vents that spew out hot water rich in chemicals have been discovered in parts of the deep ocean floors of the Pacific and Atlantic Oceans. The brown-looking material is made up of microbes, called bacteria, which create food from the chemicals. These bacteria are, in turn, food for tube worms (the white animals) and other creatures.

THE OCEAN DEPTHS

657 FEET

3282 FEET

13,128 FEET

JOURNEY INTO THE DEEP

From the window of a submersible you would see how life changes as you descend. The clearly-lit surface reveals an abundance of life, with numerous fish, both small and large. But as you pass through the twilight zone, and you switch on your submersible's search lights, you would notice fewer and fewer fish swimming by. In the cold, black depths of the dark zone and beyond, the powerful beams show only fleeting glimpses of creatures. If you turned off the powerful lights you might see tiny, moving pin points of light – the light produced in the skin of some animals, called bioluminescence.

In Sunlit Waters

The upper regions of the oceans are full of life. Here the sunlight is able to penetrate the water, providing the essential energy plants need to change the chemicals in the sea water into food in a process called photosynthesis. Apart from the community of animals that live around the deep ocean vents (see page 7), the basis of the food chain for all the life in the oceans are the phytoplankton, microscopic plants that bloom in the sunlit waters. These are grazed on by tiny animals called zooplankton, which, in turn, are food for larger animals.

ZOOPLANKTON

Huge numbers of zooplankton float among the phytoplankton. These animals are joined by the larvae of crabs and lobsters, as well as mollusks, small shrimps, and swimming crabs. They feed on the phytoplankton, on each other, or both. This drifting flourish of life is called plankton, and it forms a rich soup on which many creatures depend for their survival.

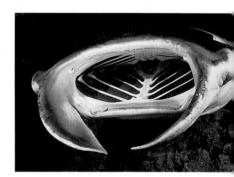

JELLYFISH

Jellyfish are invertebrates—creatures without a backbone. This compass jellyfish (left) floats near the surface of the ocean, often in large, wind-drifted groups near the coast. The long tentacles have stingers for catching fish and other animals that stray into them. Some jellyfish are well known for their powerful stingers. For example, the box jellyfish of Australasia can kill a person in less than five minutes. As a defense against the stingers, Australian lifeguards used to wear oversized women's tights pulled up over their bodies.

FLOATING RAFTS OF WEED

Great yellowish rafts of Sargassum weed survive in the Sargasso Sea in the Atlantic Ocean, buoyed up by small air bladders. The weed originally comes from weed beds in shallow, tropical waters. But during storms it floats out into the open ocean. Soon it begins to attract a wide variety of creatures (see page 27).

PARROT FISH

A regal parrot fish nips off pieces of coral using its sharp, beak-like teeth, and then grinds up the hard mouthful with its back teeth to extract the polyps (see page 18).

Coral reefs are famed for their abundance of colorful fish. The bright hues make the fish stand out when they swim around the reef, but are good camouflage when they dive for safety among the corals themselves.

HEADS UP

Garden eels live in the huge expanses of sand that cover the ocean floor near the edges of the continents. They bury their tails in the sand and, with their heads held up, feed on particles of food carried in the currents that sweep across the sand.

WIDE-MOUTHED FISH

The manta ray's diet of plankton is so nourishing that it can grow to an incredible 23 feet (7 m) across and weigh over 1.5 tons. On either side of its head are flipper-like scoops that channel the food into its wide mouth. The plankton are caught on combs as the water leaves its throat through slits on the sides of its head.

PACKED TOGETHER

A shoal of sardines feeds on the living broth of plankton. These and other small fish, such as herring, anchovy, and flying fish, are hunted by marine predators, including mackerel, that are only slightly bigger than their prey. By swimming together the sardines follow one another in their search for food-rich waters. Large shoals also make it difficult for hunters to choose which fish to attack first.

THE TWILIGHT ZONE

The further you descend, the darker and colder the oceans get. The light fades rapidly and soon it becomes close to freezing. Algae do not grow here, so food is scarce. But there is a steady rain of debris—the bodies of creatures and droppings—drifting slowly downward from the surface, and this provides a ready meal for the zooplankton, prawns, and fish living in this twilight zone. Many creatures have developed large eyes so that they can see in the dim light, and their bodies are often colored red, drab brown, or black, providing excellent camouflage in the gloom. Most creatures also produce their own light, generated by light-producing organs called photophores. Sometimes the lights are on the underside of their bodies so that the creatures are less visible. Some animals spend the hours of daylight in the safety of the twilight zone, but come up to shallower waters to feed at night.

SPONGES

These sponges live on the bottom of the oceans. They filter out food particles by drawing in water through small pores and passing it out through larger holes. Food becomes scarcer and scarcer the deeper you go. With so little nourishment available, it can take a long time for the deeper-dwelling animals to grow to full maturity.

DAGGER TOOTHED

The viperfish's mouth has dagger-like teeth for grabbing its prey. The lower jaw is bigger than the top jaw, because the bottom teeth are so long—in fact, they do not fit into the mouth when it is closed. Inside the mouth are light organs that the fish uses to lure its prey to its death. The jaws hinge open very wide to allow the fish to swallow its meal.

SQUIDS

These torpedo-shaped animals are among the most common creatures living in the sea. This one has organs along its body to light its way in the deep water. Because of the huge pressure of the water on the bodies of creatures that live far below the surface, many of them are small. However, there are exceptions: the giant squid, which lives at depths of up to 3,280 feet (1,000 m), can grow up to 66 feet (20 m) long.

SEA LILY

At first sight you might be mistaken in believing that this was a plant. In fact, it is an animal, called a crinoid, or sea lily. Its delicate "leaves" are feathery arms encircling the mouth. This one is on a shallow coral reef, but others are found at much greater depths, living in the deep sea and trenches.

BOGGLE EYES & WIDE MOUTH

The hatchet fish is so-called because of its deep belly, which gives it the appearance of a small axe. The bulbous eyes are specially designed for seeing in the extremely poor light, and are many times more sensitive to light than the human eye. Some hatchet fish look upward, hoping to see the outline of their prey against the light from above, and then catch it in their wide mouths. Right is the skeleton of a hatchet fish, with its bones stained red.

THE DEEP OCEAN

No light from the sun ever reaches below 3,280 feet (1,000 m). Consequently, it is completely black. Since much of the rain of debris is eaten higher up, there is hardly any food and so there are fewer animals at the greater depths. The abyssal plain, down to 19,690 ft (6,000 m), is covered in a layer of ooze. This mud-like carpet can be very thick—hundreds of feet deep in some places—and is very soft. Scattered on some parts of the ocean floor are nodules—hard, round lumps of minerals, such as manganese, nickel, and iron. Some are the size of cherries, others as large as grapefruits. They are not washed there by the currents, but form in very deep water. The nodules are valuable, and humans try to extract them by dredging.

ANGLER FISH

This ferocious-looking fish with its sharp teeth and wide gape has a lure on the top of its head. The lure is on a long spine, and its glow tricks other fish into thinking it is food. If one is foolish enough to be attracted by the lure, the angler fish quickly sucks it up whole into its large mouth. A female angler fish is up to 20 times larger than the male fish. In order to mate, the small male uses his teeth to attach himself to her body close to her reproductive opening. Remarkably, his body begins to fuse with her body, and eventually his heart wastes away as his bloodstream is replaced by hers. He is no longer able to swim away but is attached forever, fertilizing her eggs for the rest of her life.

MOUTH FOR GULPING

The gulper eel lives up to its name. To catch its prey, it swims slowly through the inky blackness with its gaping mouth open wide. When it runs into a small fish or shrimp, it immediately snaps its mouth shut and gulps down its prey before it has time to escape.

FISH WITH STILTS

The tripod fish has a special adaptation for its life at the bottom of the ocean— long stilts for standing or moving across the ooze. The thin stilts are like stiff filaments—one each on its two pelvic fins and one on its tail fin, making a tripod—that help the fish to stay clear of the soft ooze and to move along without stirring up the bottom into clouds of particles. This fish also has long antennae to help it "see" in the gloom.

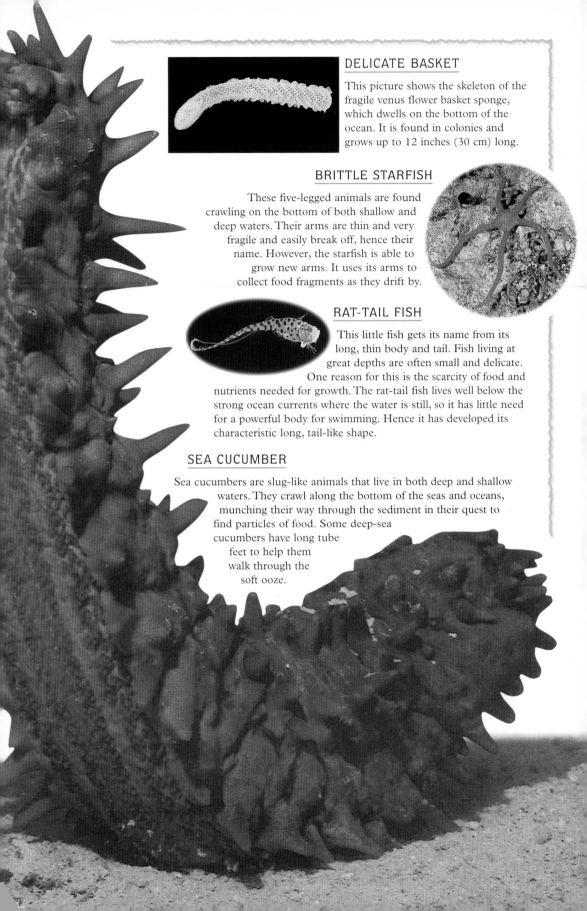

DELICATE BASKET

This picture shows the skeleton of the fragile venus flower basket sponge, which dwells on the bottom of the ocean. It is found in colonies and grows up to 12 inches (30 cm) long.

BRITTLE STARFISH

These five-legged animals are found crawling on the bottom of both shallow and deep waters. Their arms are thin and very fragile and easily break off, hence their name. However, the starfish is able to grow new arms. It uses its arms to collect food fragments as they drift by.

RAT-TAIL FISH

This little fish gets its name from its long, thin body and tail. Fish living at great depths are often small and delicate. One reason for this is the scarcity of food and nutrients needed for growth. The rat-tail fish lives well below the strong ocean currents where the water is still, so it has little need for a powerful body for swimming. Hence it has developed its characteristic long, tail-like shape.

SEA CUCUMBER

Sea cucumbers are slug-like animals that live in both deep and shallow waters. They crawl along the bottom of the seas and oceans, munching their way through the sediment in their quest to find particles of food. Some deep-sea cucumbers have long tube feet to help them walk through the soft ooze.

IN THE DARK

The deep ocean is a very inhospitable place: no sunlight ever reaches below 3,280 feet (1,000 m), the temperature of the water is icy cold, food is scarce and the pressure of thousands of tons of water is so great it would crush a diver in an instant should he go that deep. The animals that live here have special adaptations to allow them to survive the harsh conditions. For example, many deep-sea predators have massive mouths for catching prey (often several times larger than themselves) and stomachs that can stretch to take the huge meals. This is necessary because encounters between animals at great depths are few, and every opportunity for a meal must be taken, however large.

COLORED GLASS

The fabulous glass jellyfish puts on a colorful display of rainbow colors. It can be found drifting in all the oceans of the world, from the sunlit surface waters down to the twilight zone. It has a transparent body shaped like a dome, and an opening that takes in food and passes out waste.

A FEROCIOUS BITE

The wicked-looking teeth of this deep-sea fish are not for ripping massive chunks out of its prey. Instead they are for trapping an unfortunate fish inside its cavernous mouth. They are bent backwards, allowing a fish to pass easily into the mouth. If its prey is very large—perhaps even larger than itself—it might not be able to close its mouth properly. Then the teeth act as a barrier, preventing the luckless fish from escaping.

NATURAL LIGHT

In the deep, dark depths the only natural light you will see is from the creatures that live there. In nearly all cases the glow comes from the photophores in their bodies. The fact that so many animals of the deep have these light organs shows that light plays a crucial role in their survival. They can be used to attract or locate prey or a mate, or to confuse an enemy. Common sites for the organs are on the side of the head, on the flank, on the underside of the body, or on the end of a fin ray.

HAPPY GO LUCKY

Because of their large mouths and strange shape, many of the carnivorous fish found in the deep look extremely odd. Below the twilight zone, few fish have swim bladders. These are air-filled sacs that allow fish to regulate their buoyancy, so that when they stop swimming they neither sink nor float upwards. Instead, deep ocean fish achieve "neutral buoyancy" largely through having thin, lightweight skeletons and muscles. They are small, too, many no more than 4 inches (10 cm) long. In the tremendous pressure of the still water they appear to hover when not swimming.

SCARLET PRAWN

Where a tiny amount of light still reaches the depths, the prawns are deep red in color. In the sunlit waters, their color would make them stand out and they would be easy prey for a hungry fish. But in the lower reaches of the twilight zone the redness of the prawn's body is effective camouflage; in the dim light, red appears black, so that the prawn blends into the background. Below the twilight zone prawns are nearly colorless—the blanket of blackness hides them from their predators and so there is no need for camouflage.

UNDERSEA GARDENS

In the sunlit waters of the oceans grow "gardens" of seaweed. Seaweed is, in fact, algae. On land, algae grow in damp or wet areas and are small. But in the oceans they are in their element. The water supports the stipe (stem) and fronds (leaves) of the seaweed, allowing some types to grow to an enormous size. Most seaweed anchors to rocks by root-like holdfasts, which grow into every crack in the rock. The holdfasts prevent it from being carried away by the waves. Seaweed is home to a large array of creatures, including fish, crabs, shrimp, and sea urchins.

FAN WORM

There are many marine animals that look rather like plants and the fan worm is one of them. It uses the tentacles of the fan to ensnare particles of food drifting in the water.

SEAWEED ZONES

Like plants on land, seaweed needs light in order to grow. Because of this it is found only in the sunlit waters. The color of seaweed gives an indication of its depth. Near the surface grow bright green seaweed, such as sea lettuce. Then comes greenish-brown seaweed, such as the wracks, followed by brown kelp and then red seaweed.

ALL WRAPPED UP

The sea otter is a familiar inhabitant of the kelp beds of the Pacific Coast of North America, where they dive for food, such as shellfish, crustaceans, and sea urchins. The sea otter collects the food and brings it to the surface where, using a stone as an anvil, it repeatedly bashes the shell until it cracks open and the otter is able to eat the tasty flesh inside. When it wants to sleep, the sea otter rolls over and over in the kelp until it is wrapped around its body. The kelp stops the sea otter from drifting away on the tide or with the wind.

KELP FORESTS

This diver is swimming through a forest of kelp off the coast of California. This large brown seaweed, found in cold seas, can grow to lengths of over 197 feet (60 m), providing shelter for the animals that live in its midst. Unlike land plants, kelp and other seaweed have no need for roots; they are able to absorb all the water and nutrients they need from the sea around them. The holdfast's function is simply to fix the seaweed to the rock.

THE COW OF THE SEA

Dugongs are also called sea cows because they graze on the sea grasses that grow around the warm, shallow waters of the Indian and Pacific Oceans. They can grow to 12 feet (3.6 m) long. They are the only vegetarian sea mammals and are very shy. From a distance, early sailors thought dugongs looked human-like, giving rise to stories about mermaids.

SEAWEED

SEA LETTUCE

WRACK

BROWN KELP

RED SEAWEED

CORAL REEFS

Coral reefs are found in warm, clear, tropical waters. The reef is made by coral polyps, small anemone-like creatures that filter the water for food. Each polyp builds itself a protective outer skeleton to live in from a substance called calcium carbonate (or limestone). As it grows it develops a filament from which sprouts another polyp, which also builds a protective skeleton for itself. Gradually, the reef grows upwards and outwards, the outer layer being made of living coral growing on the skeletons of dead members of the colony. Living within the polyps are tiny algae, which are essential for the polyps' growth. The algae depend on the sun for photosynthesis, so coral reefs do not grow below about 490 feet (150 m). A great many creatures make their homes in or on the reef, creating one of the richest wildlife communities found anywhere in nature.

HARD & SOFT

There are both hard corals, made by polyps with a hard outer skeleton (left), and soft corals, built by polyps with a hard internal skeleton (right). The strange shapes of reef corals give rise to some equally strange names: stag's horn, brain, sea fan, dead man's fingers, and organ coral, for example. Corals come in many different colors. Hard corals, such as stag horn, are white because of their hard outer skeletons. But the soft corals are often brightly colored yellow, red, green, black, or blue.

DEADLY BEAUTY

Do not touch this attractive fish—it is one of the most poisonous creatures in the sea. The lionfish's lacy spines house venom that can leave nasty and painful wounds. The splendid display is a warning to predators not to tamper with the fish.

REEF BUILDING

Erskine Reef is part of the Great Barrier Reef, which stretches for 1,200 miles (2,000 km) down the northeast coast of Australia. It was built by creatures the size of a pinhead over a period of several million years. The small, low island, called a cay, is made up of fragments of coral. In the Pacific, reefs often form a ring around volcanic islands. These are called fringing reefs and the water inside the reefs is called a lagoon. Atolls are circular reefs or strings of coral islands surrounding a lagoon.

RECORD BREAKER

The giant clam has the largest shell on Earth. It can grow to over 3 feet (1 m) wide and weigh a quarter of a ton. This giant, filter-feeding mollusk is one of the largest animals without a backbone.

TINY TENTACLES

Coral polyps have tentacles with which to catch plankton. The tentacles, which form rings around the mouth of the animal, have darts which sting their prey. During the day, the stalks of the polyps are retracted into the protective skeletons, making the coral look like dead rock. At night they spread their tentacles to feed.

CROWN-OF-THORNS

This large, spiky-looking starfish feeds on the coral polyps. It does a great deal of damage and has destroyed large areas of Australia's Great Barrier Reef.

GREAT WHITE SHARK

TUNA

ANCHOVIES

ZOOPLANKTON

PHYTOPLANKTON

At the top of the marine food chain are the large hunters, such as sharks. These eat large fish that catch smaller fish, which in turn rely on zooplankton. The zooplankton eat the phytoplankton. Therefore the small plants that make food through photosynthesis are the basis of all life in the oceans.

PREDATORS & PREY

T he deadly game of attack and defense is played out at every level of the ocean. Creatures are constantly on the lookout for prey. But there is no such thing as an easy meal, for no creature—however large or small—wants to end up as lunch for another animal. Some animals, such as the poisonous lionfish (page 19), have bright warning colors that tell a predator to keep clear of its poisonous spines. But other animals must take evasive action if they are to survive an attack.

JET POWERED

Scallops have a unique way of escaping the deadly clutches of a hungry starfish. They use jet power to launch themselves off the bottom of the ocean, and swim away by squeezing a jet of water out of their shells. Unlike most other mollusks of their type, scallops do not bury themselves in the sand or fix themselves to the rocky bed, and so are able to escape a marauding predator.

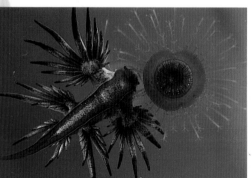

NO ESCAPE

Even the stinging cells on the tentacles of the jelly-like *Porpita* (right) are no defense for the sea slug, *Glaucus*, a type of shell-less mollusk. The sea slug crawls along the underside of the water surface looking for *Porpita*, and when it finds one it immediately starts feeding on it, stings and all.

DEADLY EMBRACE

The flower-like sea anemone, with its colorful "petals," looks pretty and innocent. But any small fish that comes too close had better beware, for the petals are armed with poisonous stinging cells. Once caught in its deadly embrace, the poor fish is pulled towards the anemone's mouth in the center of the ring of tentacles.

UNDERWATER FLIGHT

Many sea birds dive into the water to catch a meal, but the Galapagos penguin chases fish under water, using its flipper-like wings to propel it through the water with speed. When fish swim in shoals, they may confuse the bird, preventing it from deciding on a catch. The flashing of their silvery bodies may also confuse the penguin for a moment, allowing the fish to escape.

KILLER ON THE ATTACK

On an Argentinian beach a killer whale attacks sea lions by charging at them in the shallows. The killer whale, an air-breathing mammal, is willing to almost beach itself in order to catch its prey. This 33-foot (10-m) predator is the only whale to prey on other whales.

TERROR OF THE OCEANS

The most feared fish in the ocean is the great white shark. This eating machine prefers seals, turtles, and large fish, but occasionally has been known to attack humans, its sharp teeth leaving terrible injuries. The shark's streamlined body shape allows it to swim effortlessly through the water, driven by its large, powerful tail. Sharks have no swim bladder so they must swim constantly to stay afloat.

MIGRATION

Animals that move from one place to another are said to migrate. For example, zooplankton make a daily migration. During the night they feed on the phytoplankton that live in the surface waters. But as day breaks they swim down several hundred feet to escape hungry predators. However, for other marine animals, migration is more commonly associated with breeding. Some fish, seals, whales, and turtles make spectacular migrations, often swimming thousands of miles on difficult journeys to lay their eggs or give birth to their offspring. They travel to a place where the young have the best chance of survival, perhaps where there are plentiful food supplies, guided on their journey by the ocean currents.

THE CONGER EEL

The conger eel of the North Atlantic is a fearless hunter. It has rows of sharp, backward-pointing teeth that grip into its prey. The only known spawning ground of the conger eel is north of the Azores. It seems that all western European congers travel here in midsummer to lay their eggs later returning to colder northern waters.

MIGRATION MYSTERY

The mystery of the European eel's breeding habits remained a puzzle until this century. Then it was discovered that the adult eels leave the rivers of Europe and swim out into the Sargasso Sea in the Atlantic Ocean, where they spawn and then die. After about three years, the young eels, or elvers, find their way to those rivers, where they remain until they, too, are ready to return to the spawning grounds in the Atlantic.

TURTLE TRAVELS

Green turtles come ashore to lay their eggs. But they do not breed on any beach they come across. Instead they travel hundreds, even thousands, of miles to the place where they hatched. Under the cover of darkness, they haul themselves high up the beach, where they use their large, powerful flippers to dig a deep nest in the soft sand. After carefully covering the eggs with sand, the females return to the sea to leave the young to fend for themselves.

WHALE OF A TIME

A southern right whale surfaces in the food-rich waters of the Southern Ocean. When it is time for the females to give birth, they migrate north to the warmer waters of their breeding grounds. There is not much food there, so the adults must survive on their reserves of blubber until they are able to return to their feeding grounds.

MARCHING IN SINGLE FILE

The spiny lobster lives close to the coast where the ocean bed is rocky. For most of the year, they hide in crevices during the day, venturing out at night to feed on worms and dead animals. But in the autumn, along the coast of Florida and the Caribbean, their behavior changes. They join together in long lines of up to 50 lobsters, each one keeping in touch with the lobster in front of it with its long antennae. They move off away from the coast into deep water, where they mate.

PRAWN LARVAE

A female prawn, called *Parapandalus*, carries her eggs stuck to her legs on the underside of her body. It lives at depths of about 1,640–2,300 feet (500–700 m) in the dim regions of the ocean. When the eggs hatch, the larvae swim up to the surface to feed on the phytoplankton. As they grow, they change their diet and start to eat other small animals. They eventually migrate down to the depths where the adults live.

Spawn & Young

A MERMAID'S PURSE

This is the name for the dried-out, empty egg cases of skates, rays and dogfish, often found washed up on the beach. Here a swell shark embryo sits on its egg case. The male fertilized the female and when the eggs developed she laid the egg cases, attaching them to seaweed by tendrils at each corner. The embryos live off the yolk sac until they have developed enough to emerge.

Many marine animals do not have elaborate courtship behavior or care for their young. When the time is right, the female simply releases her eggs into the water while the male fertilizes them with his sperm. The eggs are left to develop on their own, and when they hatch the young grow and develop without the help of their parents. However, the eggs and young are food for a great many animals. So hundreds, even thousands, of eggs are often laid by one animal in order that at least a few individuals survive to adulthood and are able to spawn (produce eggs) themselves. There are some exceptions to this rule. Like other mammals, whales are good examples of animals that take good care of their young. When they are born, the calves are helped to the surface to take their first breath. They drink their mothers' milk for many months and are protected from predators by the adults.

DESPERATE DASH

Loggerhead turtle hatchlings head for the relative safety of the ocean. The mother loggerhead laid her eggs in the sand about two months earlier. As the babies emerge from the sand, it is the most dangerous part of their young lives, for they are easy prey for sea birds, crabs and other predators.

So as soon as they hatch, they scramble as fast as possible to the ocean. One day they will return to the beach where they were born to lay eggs of their own.

BRAIN SPAWN

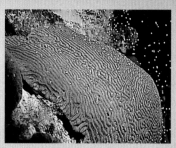

Coral reefs start when tiny planktonic larvae settle in warm shallow water where they become polyps (see page 18). The larvae develop when a coral, such as this brain coral, releases packets of eggs and sperm into the water.

PUPPY LOVE

Not all fish lay eggs. Some sharks do lay eggs, but most sharks breed like whales and other mammals and give birth to live young. After mating with the male, the female carries an embryo which develops inside her body. When it is fully formed she gives birth to the infant shark, which looks exactly like an adult but much smaller. Here a lemon shark pup is being born.

ROLE REVERSAL

Unusually, it is the male sea horse that becomes pregnant and gives birth to the young. The female lays her eggs in a pouch in the male's body, using a tube called an ovipositor, and then leaves him to look after them. Several weeks later the baby sea horses hatch and are ready to be born. Then the male begins to convulse forwards and backwards, and with each backwards movement a baby shoots out of the pouch. He gives birth to around 200 baby sea horses.

SOLE METAMORPHOSIS

The sole is a type of flatfish that, in early life, goes through an extraordinary change. One eye migrates around the head as the fish changes shape.

TEN DAYS OLD **THIRTEEN DAYS OLD** **TWENTY-TWO DAYS OLD** **ADULT SOLE**

LIVING TOGETHER

MATING GAME

A large school of squid torpedoes around in order to find a mate. These fast-moving animals hunt together, using their large eyes to seek out a shoal of fish. Squid use their 10 sucker-covered tentacles to grasp their prey—or a mate. Squid can move forward or backward through the water. They have two methods of propulsion. With the first, the squid sucks water into its body and then squirts it out of a tube at high speed; the force of the water-jet shoots it through the ocean. The second method is slower: the squid moves by waving the fin at the rear of its body.

Throughout the oceans, there are creatures that live together, often forming close relationships. These relationships do not happen by chance—there is always a reason for them. Some animals of the same kind band together and swim in large shoals as a defense against predators, or to improve their chances of catching a meal. Other relationships involve animals of very different kinds, each creature providing some form of benefit for the other. This type of relationship is called "symbiosis." In the case of coral polyps, the symbiotic relationship is between the polyps and the algae living within them (see page 18).

CLOWNING AROUND

A clownfish finds refuge among the stinging tentacles of a sea anemone that would paralyze other fish in seconds: the clownfish's body is covered in a mucus that renders it immune to the sea anemone's stings. In return, the sea anemone benefits from the bits that are left over from its guest's meal, or by capturing predators that are drawn to attack the clownfish and instead end up in the anemone's deadly embrace.

HAPPY HERMIT

This hermit crab crawls along the sea bed. The shell in which it is living, and which protects its soft, vulnerable body, once belonged to a mollusk. And on the shell it has placed anemones whose stinging tentacles provide the hermit crab with protection against predators. In return, the anemones get to feed on food particles left over from the crab's meals.

FLOATING FLOTSAM

Living among the floating Sargassum weed and drifting with it are many different animals, including sea slugs, crabs, shrimps, and goose barnacles, all cleverly adapted to their special habitat. Here a small fish with fleshy growths blends in with the weed, making it almost invisible to predators. A sea anemone sits nearby waiting for a fish to swim into its stinging tentacles. Both creatures are using color as camouflage, allowing them to blend in with the weed.

CLEANING SERVICE

Cleaner wrasses give the inside of a large cod's mouth a wash and brush up without being harmed. The wrasses help the cod (and other fish) by removing parasites or particles of food; in return they get a free meal.

HITCHING A RIDE

A remora hitches a ride on a manta ray. The remora has a sucker on the top of its head that it uses to attach itself to the larger fish. Remoras are often seen on sharks, disengaging themselves to feed on the scraps of a kill.

PEOPLE & THE OCEAN

TOURIST TRAP

A scuba diver admires the inhabitants of a coral reef. Foreign holidays in the sun are now immensely popular, with the majority of people visiting destinations on the coast. Sun bathing, fishing trips, sailing, and diving are just a few of the popular activities offered at holiday resorts. While tourism brings welcome money for the local population and a better standard of living, it does have its dangers for the environment.

People have always been involved with the oceans, depending on them at first for food, and then later for mineral wealth. People have fished for thousands of years, and today it remains a major occupation in both the developing world and richer countries. Mining of the sea is important too. For example, the age-old extraction of salt from sea water has been joined by the dredging of sand and gravel, and the drilling for oil and gas (shown here). Tourism has become a major industry too, and in many traditional coastal communities this has replaced fishing as the main source of income.

FISH HARVEST

This Scottish fishing boat is bringing its catch aboard. Day and night, large fishing boats all around the world reap the bounty of the oceans in an attempt to satisfy the rising demand for fish. With more powerful boats, improved technology, and bigger nets, they are able to remain at sea longer, and bring home bigger catches. In order to avoid overfishing and depleting stocks of fish, there are international treaties which set precise limits on the size of a country's catch.

DIVING FOR PEARLS

A pearl diver in Thailand brings his catch of oysters to the surface. The pearls are formed around a foreign body, such as a grain of sand, inside the shell of an oyster or mussel, and take several years to grow. Pearl diving is difficult and dangerous work. This diver is using make-shift diving equipment made from a generator and some rubber tubing. Pearls are much valued as gems and so the money the diver makes from selling them makes the job worth the risk.

STILT FISHERMEN

In traditional societies methods of fishing have not changed in hundreds of years. Here a Sri Lankan fisherman perches patiently on his stilt while waiting for a bite. For people in coastal villages in poor countries, the oceans are often the only source of food. For many people it is their livelihood, but often it is under threat from foreign fishing boats that take the local fish stocks.

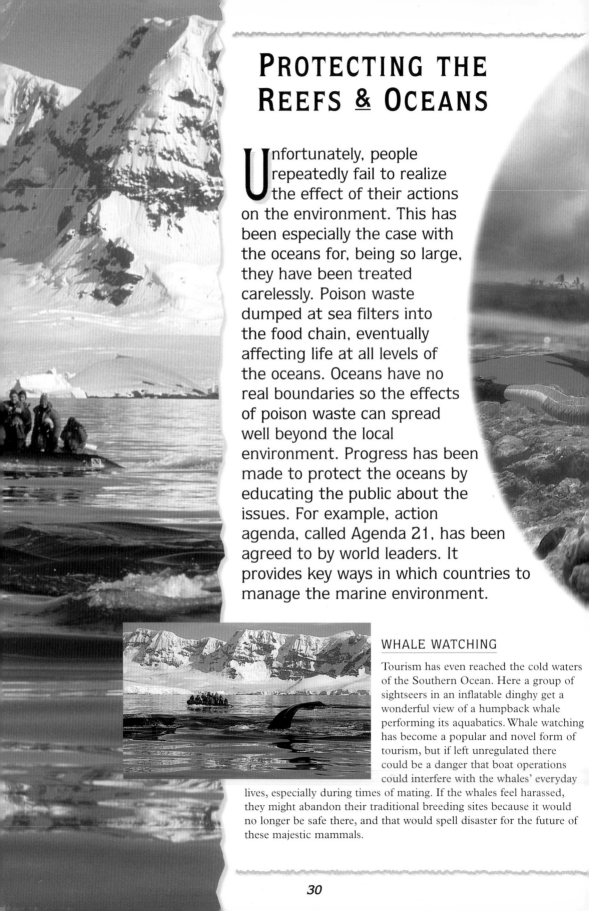

PROTECTING THE REEFS & OCEANS

Unfortunately, people repeatedly fail to realize the effect of their actions on the environment. This has been especially the case with the oceans for, being so large, they have been treated carelessly. Poison waste dumped at sea filters into the food chain, eventually affecting life at all levels of the oceans. Oceans have no real boundaries so the effects of poison waste can spread well beyond the local environment. Progress has been made to protect the oceans by educating the public about the issues. For example, action agenda, called Agenda 21, has been agreed to by world leaders. It provides key ways in which countries to manage the marine environment.

WHALE WATCHING

Tourism has even reached the cold waters of the Southern Ocean. Here a group of sightseers in an inflatable dinghy get a wonderful view of a humpback whale performing its aquabatics. Whale watching has become a popular and novel form of tourism, but if left unregulated there could be a danger that boat operations could interfere with the whales' everyday lives, especially during times of mating. If the whales feel harassed, they might abandon their traditional breeding sites because it would no longer be safe there, and that would spell disaster for the future of these majestic mammals.

TURTLE HATCHERY

In many countries, turtle eggs are a delicacy. On the nights when the animals come ashore to breed, local people patrol the beaches and collect the eggs for sale in the local markets. Some countries have made an effort to protect the eggs. In Sri Lanka, green turtle eggs are placed in a hatchery for protection and the baby turtles released directly into the ocean.

PROTECTING THE REEFS

Some coral reefs have been made marine nature reserves, to protect them from overexploitation, such as the plundering of coral, sponges, and shells for sale to tourists, or the collection of fish for pet stores. People have found other ways of developing tourism in these places, creating local jobs without harming the delicate reef environment.

DOLPHIN DELIGHT

Despite being wild, the bottlenose dolphins at Monkey Mia in Western Australia come into the shallows to seek human contact. This interaction allows us to study the wild dolphins, in the hope of understanding more about them. There are just under 40 species of dolphins, but several are threatened by fishing nets, overfishing, and pollution.

CLEANING UP

Pollution is one of the main threats to the marine environment. To tackle the problem, laws have been passed to ban tankers from cleaning out their tanks, and dumping dangerous waste, such as radioactive waste, at sea. Measures are also being taken by many countries to reduce pollution from land-based sources, such as untreated sewage and toxic chemicals dumped into rivers that eventually flow into the oceans.

FIND OUT MORE

Useful Addresses and Websites

To find out more about life in the ocean, or theprotection of marine wildlife, here are someorganizations who may be able to help.

CENTER FOR MARINE CONSERVATION
1725 DeSales Street, Suite 600
Washington, DC 20036
(202) 429-5609 http:/www.cmc-ocean.org/

CENTER FOR OCEANIC RESEARCH & EDUCATION
245 Western Avenue, Box 8
Essex, MA 01929
http:/www.coreresearch.org/

FRIENDS OF THE EARTH
1025 Vermont Avenue, NW, 3rd Floor
Washington, DC 20005
(202) 783-7400 http:/www.foe.org/

GREENPEACE
1436 U Street, NW
Washington, DC 20009
1-800-326-0959 http:/www.greenpeaceusa.org/

OCEANIC RESOURCE FOUNDATION
P.O. Box 280216
San Francisco, CA 94128
1-888-835-9478 participate@orf.org

REEF ENVIRONMENTAL EDUCATION FOUNDATION
P.O. Box 246, Key Largo, FL 33037
http:/www.reef.org/

SEACOAST INFORMATION SERVICES, INC.
135 Auburn Drive
Charlestown, RI 02813
(401) 364-9916 http:/www.aquanet.com

First edition for the United States, its territories and dependencies, Canada and the Philippine Republic, published 1999 by
Barron's Educational Series, Inc.
Original edition copyright © by 1999 Ticktock Publishing, Ltd.
U.S. edition copyright © 1999 by Barron's Educational Series, Inc.

All inquiries should be addressed to:
Barron's Educational Series, Inc., 250 Wireless Boulevard, Hauppauge, New York 11788
http://www.barronseduc.com
Library of Congress Catalog Card No. 98-74674
International Standard Book No. 0-7641-0641-4
Printed in Hong Kong
987654321

Picture Credits: t=top, b=bottom, c=center, l=left, r=right, OFC=outside front cover, OBC=outside back cover, IFC=inside front cover

Andy Crump/Still Pictures; 5b. BBC Natural History Unit; 16b. B&C Alexander; 22/23t. Bruce Coleman Limited; 6bl, 26ct, 31tr.
Innerspace Visions; OFC (main pic), 20/21b. Michel Freeman/Auscape; 28/29ct. NHPA; 12tl, 24/25 (main pic). Oxford Scientific Films; 2bl,
4tl, 5cr, 8cl, 9bl, 11cr, 13cr, 14tl, 17tr, 18l & 18cl, 18/19cb, 19tr, 20tl, 20cl, 20br, 22/23c, 26l, & 26bl & OCB, 27tr, 27cr, 27br, 28tl,
29ct, 30l & 30bl, 30/31c. Planet Earth Pictures; OFC (inset pic), OBC, IFC, 2l & 2cl, 2/3c, 3cr, 3br, 4bl, 5tr, 6/7 (main pic); 6/7cb, 6/7ct, 8l,
8cr, 8/9c, 9cr, 10tl, 10bl, 10/11cb, 11br, 12bl, 12br, 12/13c, 13t, 13cl, 15tr, 15br, 16tl, 17c, 17tl & 32, 18/19ct, 19br, 21b, 22tr, 22b,
23b, 23tr, 24tl, 24/25ct, 25tr, 25c, 26/27, 28bl, 30/31cb, 31cr. Telegraph Colour Picture Library: 6tl, 14bl, 14/15c, 18/19c.
Tony Stone; 28/29 (main pic).

Every effort has been made to trace the copyright holders and we apologize in advance for any unintentional omissions.
We would be pleased to insert the appropriate acknowledgment in any subsequent edition of this publication.